MARK-
DAVID tells
me you're
A legend
+ WOULD
DiE
This
i Merli

D1592773

IT'S HARD TO BE A

PERSON

by

Brett Newski

NOMAD UNION   ramshackle
press

IT'S HARD TO BE A PERSON:
Defeating Anxiety, Surviving the World, and Having More Fun

by Brett Newski

Artwork and Words: Brett Newski

Published and Distributed by:

Nomad Union
Milwaukee/Toronto/Cape Town

AND

ramshackle press
Viroqua, WI

Copy Editor: Anna Sacks
Layout Editor: Parker Forsell

ISBN: 978-0-578-87554-5

First edition
Created in Wisconsin
Printed in Illinois

for anna...

INTRO

Years ago, somewhere on the Internet, I posted a few dumb drawings making fun of my own anxiety and depression. The response to them was warmer than anticipated, and people kept asking for more. Blending humor with pure depression seemed to strike a chord with a decent amount of people. So I kept going, and after about three years of drawing, I had enough dumb drawings for a book.

Mental health is a serious thing, and it gets heavier when humans don't talk about it outwardly. I bottled up feelings for many years. Feelings I considered "dark", "weak", "downhearted", "embarrassing", "shameful" or any number of self-deprecating words. But after saying (or drawing) them out loud to people, all that weight went away and I realized these feelings were just part of being a person.

Humor has always been a primary mode of therapy for me. I still make fun of my own anxiety and depression. It's cathartic for me. I sing about it on tour, talk about it on my podcast, and draw pictures of it here in this book. Putting my formerly-private-feelings out into the world has been tremendous therapy for me, and I wish I would've done it sooner.

So, I've been illustrating the "hacks", "strategies", or "exercises" that have worked best for me in combating the struggles in my head.

I'm not a doctor, just a person who spends too much time in his own head. More than anything I want this book to be useful for people. The objective of *It's Hard to Be a Person* is not to give unsolicited advice, but to hopefully save you some headaches on the long n' winding road of life in your brain.

"I will always appreciate bad days like this,
because they grant me a point of reference
in regards to my happiness." -Sean Bonnette (AJJ)

Chapter One:
Defeating Anxiety

Anxiety gets a negative rep. Somewhere along the line, anxiety was deemed BAD. In actuality, anxiety is useful energy. It is untapped creative fuel. It is there for a reason.

Yes, anxiety can be crippling in large doses. I've certainly gone down "the toilet bowl of panic" in my head. However, when anxiety is managed properly it can be mined as energy to spawn fresh ideas, conversations, creative projects and any number of inspirations.

When I experience calm after feeling anxious, I go back to analyze my anxious thoughts from before. Most often, I'll realize that none of those thoughts were even close to rational. Ninety nine percent of the things I worry about aren't even reasonable worries. The brain can become a hall of mirrors where negative thoughts bounce off one another and multiply.

This chapter is my take on anxiety and how to keep it in check and use it to your advantage.

What **anxiety** and **depression** want you to do...

Not tell anyone

Stay inside

Judge your body

Magnify fear

Doubt yourself

Lose all patience

Distort reality

Stay on the couch

Take blame

How to **not freak out**
in a busy social setting.

Focus only on 1-2
people the whole night.

Have an "ice breaker"
question ready
in your back pocket.

Step outside for air to
recharge social battery.

Don't be afraid of
having pre-planned
talking points.

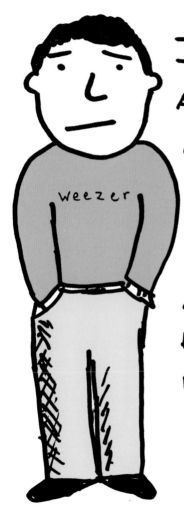

If you're feeling a little nervous or anxious at a social event, remember that almost everyone else feels that way too.

What to do when you get **trapped** in your own **brain.**

Remember you are not your **brain.**

Talk to your brain as if it were another person and make **friends** with it.

Remember to not do this in **public.**

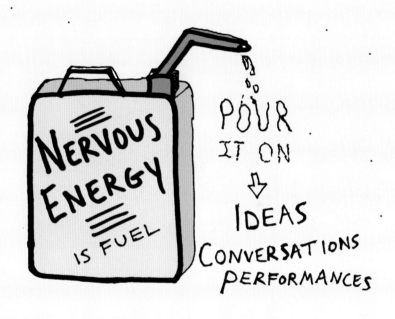

I'M NOT
MY MIND.
I NEVER WAS
I'M NOT
THE THINGS
THAT I AM
THINKING OF.

How to **"break the ice"** with new people.

Say "hello" in a different or more unique way.

Liken them to a cool celebrity.

Compliment.

Find commonalities and try to involve everyone.

Me before almost
any social event.

Great rule for joining conversations.

If there are only **two people** talking, don't interrupt.

If there are **three or more people** it's ok to join the circle by saying "do you guys mind if I join the circle?"

credit tim ferris.

Places to **avoid** because they may trigger **anxiety.**

Environment is crucial to mental health.

Arby's

Arby's

DRIVE THRU

SOCIAL MEDIA

NEW BERLIN WEST
HIGH SCHOOL REUNION!

N/A
BEER

POPSicles

SODA

Percent of people who experience **self-doubt**

Ways to relieve stress.

OPTION #1

Win a sauna
from a daytime TV
infomercial.

OPTION #2

Go to YMCA and
sit in the sauna.

Ways to relieve stress, part II
Styles for smashing acoustic **guitars**.

Tomahawk.

Jackhammer.

Stone Cold Steve Austin.

Fargo.

Ways to relieve stress.

Part III

BASEBALL CAR MASSAGE

rind a baseball on your
back while you drive.

INTERNATIONAL SALAD DAY

Eat only salad
for one day.

YUM YUM YUM

Switch to decaf
for a day or two or many.

FIRE ALL SODA FROM LIFE

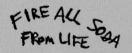

Poison.

TOE TOUCH NINJA STRETCH

Stretching is my #1

If you're afraid of **swimming** in lakes or oceans.

View the statistics that you're more likely to get struck by **lightning** than attacked by a **shark**.

Don't swim in the ocean.

Swim in a **karate suit** so sharks know not to mess with you.

One way to overcome the **fear of death.**

Just recall what it was like

before you were born.

It wasn't bad at all.

paraphrased from chris ryan. inspired by walter salas-humara.

When **someone** doesn't reply to your **email**.

STEP 1

Follow up after a few days.

STEP 2

Do this with your hands because people are **busy,** the **world** is insane, and **email isn't** even real anyway.

How to avoid going **insane** from Social Media

OPTION #1

Unfollow those who make you feel bad.

OPTION #2

Throw phone in river.

Alternative communication options when your smartphone drives you insane.

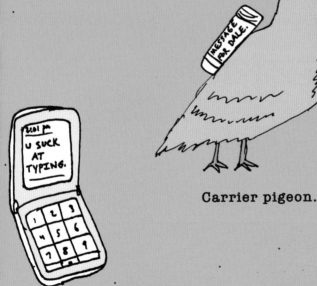

Carrier pigeon.

Flip phone.

Talk directly to another human's face.

How to Achieve **Privacy**.

Light iPhone
on **fire**.

Smash phone
with **hammer**.

Work for
WikiLeaks,
living in
secret asylum
in a
foreign embassy.

Why it's important to **not compare** yourself to others online.

Part I.

No one takes the exact same path.

People's lives online are a smokescreen.

"Comparison is the thief of joy." - Teddy Roosevelt

Why it's important to **not compare** yourself to others online.

Part II.

It completely derails you from your mission.

Looking at too many selfies induces nausea.

If you are **worried** someone is mad at you...

Ask them.

Know that they are likely going thru their own stuff and it has **nothing** to do with **you**.

Quick ways to relieve **stress.**

Part III

OPTION 1

Dunk & shatter
the backboard.

OPTION 2

If you can't dunk just
clean your room real nice.

inspired by vonnie kyle.

8 **albums** to pull you out of a depression.

Obviously music is subjective, but here are my picks!

"MAKERS" BY
Rocky VOTOLATO

"TRAMP" BY
SHARON VAN ETTEN

"CANT MAINTAIN"
AJJ

"SORRY IS GONE"
BY JESSICA LEA MAYFIELD

"BANGING DOWN THE DOORS"
BY EZRA FURMAN

"LOVE IRE + SONG"
BY FRANK TURNER

"GANGING UP ON THE SUN"
BY GUSTER

FELICE BROTHERS
FIRST ALBUM

What to do if you drank **too much caffeine**.

Jog or walk with a **hoodie** to sweat more.

Lift weights.

Buy and install adjustable basketball hoop in driveway & **dunk** until buzz wears off.

When it feels like **everyone** in the world is making **progress** but you.

Take **multiple days off** social media.

Take an **afternoon drive** to the countryside.

Make a note of your **tiny victories** over the past year.

Good things to do when **feeling lonely.**

part 1

Call a **buddy**
even if you don't feel
like it.

Remember there are
billions of people
who feel the same.

Walk/wrestle/rub
someone's **dog**
(but ask first).
There are **apps**
for this.

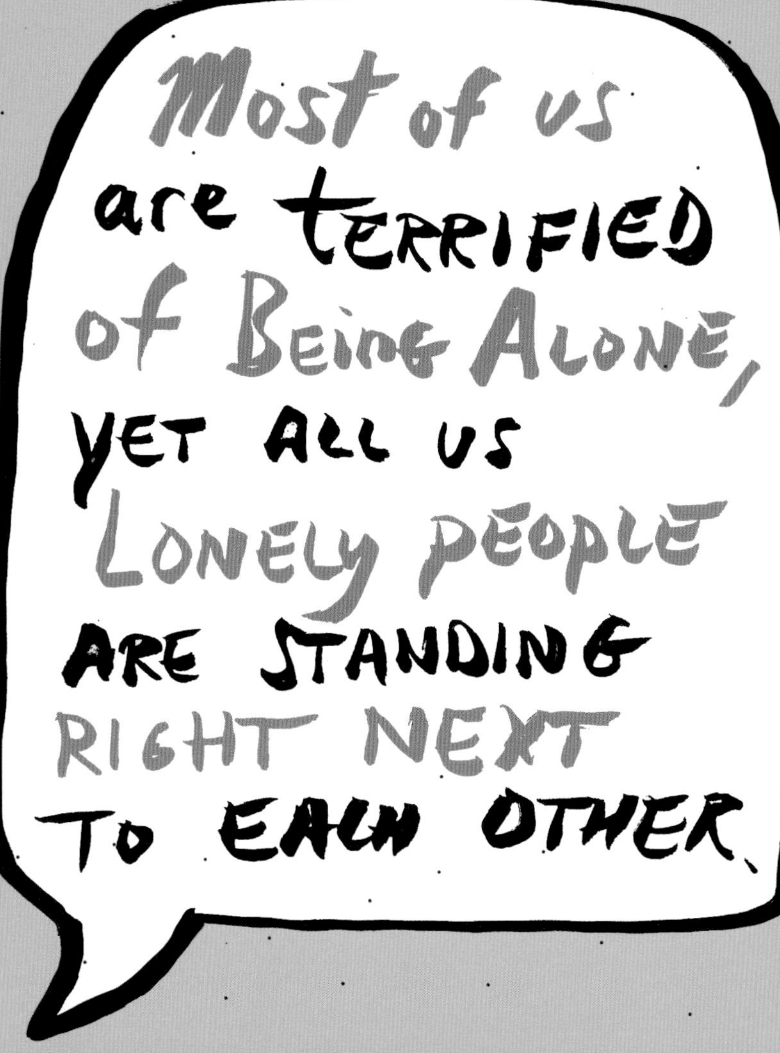
Most of us
are TERRIFIED
of BEING ALONE,
YET ALL US
LONELY PEOPLE
ARE STANDING
RIGHT NEXT
TO EACH OTHER.

Good things to do when feeling lonely.

part II

Create something that didn't exist before
(poem, song, drawing, etc)

Plan a one-day **road trip** with a buddy.

Take an evening and randomly call people who would enjoy hearing from you: old friends, cousins, 2nd cousins, weird uncles, parents, elders you respect.

When you're Down & Out, It's normal to feel like you'll be stuck there forever. Please note, Everything is Temporary.

WE WERE
BUILT
TO MOVE ON.

"You can't forget that you're ALIVE."
-Joe Strummer

CHAPTER TWO:
SURVIVING THE WORLD

The world is an unmetered taxi ordering drive-thru at McInsanity. What I'm trying to say is that "civilized" human life on the planet earth is totally nuts.

New obstacles are always darting out of the nooks and crannies of life: Health scares, financial wobbles, misinformation, bullies, dating, tough bosses, grouchy neighbors, and the constant inner battle with oneself. That's why the most cliche song lyric of all time is "SAVE ME FROM MYSELF". :)

This section of the book offers ideas for "surviving the world".

When **doors slam** in your face.

Go to the **next** door.
(there are always more doors)

How to ward off a slimy used **car salesman**

Pick up fake **emergency** phone call and walk away.

Throw a **decoy wallet** over your shoulder and run.

Sprinkle foul smelling **fish food** in a circle around you and **light it on fire.**

Meaningless things you can say that sound better than **"um."**

"Having said that, ..."

"Understand, ..."

"Now, ..."

"Getting back to my point..."

Products that should exist, **but don't.**

Only $1.99 !

CHEAPEST "ON-THE-GO" MEALS FOR A Happy Brain

PLAIN YOGURT + NUTS

TWO (2) HARD-BOILED EGGS.

PEANUT BUTTER & BANANA.

How to avoid eating fast food

Read ingredients list.

Remember the pain it caused you last time.

Watch viral video of drunk David Hasselhoff eating cheeseburgers off the floor.

How to boost national health.

Make a **law** that requires lead-ingredient
to be the **brand** name.

How to **save** the polar bears.

Feed them
climate change
deniers.

Vices that are good for morale when you need a "pick me up".

Ice cream.

Small
ice coffee.

Journey
(the band)

When someone **cuts you off** in **traffic** and you get angry.

Let them **pass**.

Embrace how **little** it means.

Remember they might have a **gun**.

When someone **invades** your personal space.

Say "I've gotta go to the **bathroom**".

Run to the bathroom.

Just go.

Things to do if You Don't Feel Like **Drinking**.

Arcade.

Hot springs.

Look for Moose.

Play fiercely competitive kickball for money.

How to deal with **grumpy** people.

"Kill them with Kindness."

Ignore them as much as possible without being impolite.

How to subdue **road rage.**

Breathe deep.

Remember it's not worth.it.

Remove Louisville Slugger from trunk & donate it to little league.

How to **escape** a person with **diarrhea-of-the-mouth**

Answer a fake phone call.

Walk away slowly, smile and wave.

Profitable, unconventional ways to make **$$$**

Hustle fools in street ball.

Open a cuddle cafe.

Work here.

High-value
rummage sale acquisitions.

Vintage
video
games.

MAD MEN
furniture.

Picture frames
where
dead relatives
hid **mad cash.**

Top 3 businesses to open if you love **bankruptcy**.

Alternative league to the **NFL**.

BASEBALL CARDS

POG Factory.

How to diffuse
a political debate.

Change subject.

Don't ever forget
option #1

How to avoid fake news.

Live in the woods and **never** speak to anyone again.

How to **prep for D-Day** caused by A.I.

Build cabin in the woods with no wifi.

Watch Terminator 2 on VHS.

Most American ways to die inside.

Devote soul
to Instagram

Acquire
corn-syrup I.V.

Buy material
goods you'll
throw away
in 6 months

How to **stomach** self-promotion.

OPTION 1

Make fun
of yourself.

OPTION 2

Make fun of
the Internet.

OPTION 3

Become a
sociopath.

Why **Facebook** pisses you off.

It engages you when you're **most vulnerable.**

It shows you anger-inducing posts because they get **more clicks.**

Your acquaintances make you look at their **sandwiches.**

How to spot **sociopaths.**

Their fake laugh
sounds like
their real laugh.

They exhibit the
1000-yard-stare
when you speak
to them.

They eat
kittens.

Products that should exist, **but don't.**

Only $2.99!

Easy ways to inject **positive** vibes into the world.

Wish your pals &
accquaintances
happy bday online

Talk to homeless folks

High-five other joggers

Ask people "what gets
you excited these days?"

"These things in human life are important: The first is to be kind; the second is to be kind; and the third is to be kind." *- **Henry James***

Types of **buddies.**

FRIEND BUDDY

LOVE BUDDY

WISE ELDER BUDDY

ONLINE BUDDIES

LITTLE BUDDY.

NON PERSON BUDDY

Quality over quantity

We don't need a ton of friends,
just one or two or three quality ones.

Types of **bullies**
to watch out for.

MACHO BULLY

MIDDLE SCHOOL Bully
GRADE-SCHOOL BULLY

CYBER BULLY

Gossip Bully

DRUNK
ALPHA BRO.

HIPSTER BULLY

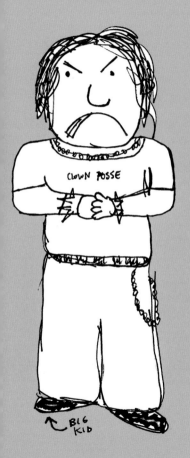

CLOWN POSSE

← BIG
  KID

WHEN
BIG MEAN PEOPLE
SAY B.S. TO YOU,
CONSIDER
THE
SOURCE.

THEY BRING NOTHING
TO THE TABLE.

Effective ways to stand up to internet **bullies**.

SILENCE

Often the best tactic.

SHARING
THE BULLIES
COMMENT PUBLICLY

Expose the bully and
show self-confidence.

WITTY
SARCASM

...if you can handle
confrontation.

KINDNESS

"Sorry you feel that way."
Short n' sweet diffuses.

STRENGTH

When a **giant**, mean-looking motorcyclist revs his **engine directly** in your face.

Smile politely.

Don't flip him off cause that could be bad.

Remember they are **little guys on the inside** and need attention too.

Quality, simple items to stash in your **car** and give to **homeless** people at **stoplights**.

Ponchos

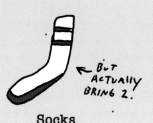

← BUT ACTUALLY BRING 2.

Socks

Sunglasses or baseball hat

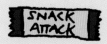

SNACK ATTACK

Mini packs of nuts, or snack bars

Philosophies on **dating**

part I

Plan to fail
(you will feel no pressure)

Think of your failures
as hilarious
(because they are)

Canned lines can be helpful
to start conversations

Being comfortable with
weakness shows strength

Premier places to **ruin** a first date.

Bro bar.

Room with your guitar collection.

High-speed batting cages.

Philosophies on **dating**

part two!

The stock quote that someone is "out of your league" is weak.

TALL
PEOPLE
DATE
SHORT
PEOPLE

WIDE
PEOPLE
DATE
NARROW
PEOPLE

BIZARRE
LOOKING
PEOPLE
DATE
GENERIC
LOOKING
PEOPLE

What to do if you think you're falling in love with a deranged person.

← MOON

Travel to a place with no cell reception.

Don't communicate for a few days **(to get clarity).**

Watch **"Fatal Attraction"** (starring Glen Close) alone in your **dark** house and think about the **aftermath/collateral** damage this releationship could leave in its wake.

Haircuts proven to **reduce** chances of getting dates.

Carrot with **frosted tips.**

Mushroom.

Bowl.

Products that should exist, but don't.

Only $1.99 !

CHAPTER 3:
HAVING MORE FUN

It took me a long long time to build up the confidence to make this book, much less release it. Procrastination cursed me thru the process. I wanted to make sure it was perfect, so I just kept staring at the pages like a lunatic. I went on tweaking tiny nuances to the point where I was losing my mind.

For years I struggled to have fun and enjoy the moment. Our band would be touring across Europe and I'd be panicked about our streaming numbers and how many tickets we'd sell. While I should've been "living the dream" in the present moment, I was constantly rattled by the future.

I lived in a perpetual state of self-avoidance to avoid the discomfort of sitting with my own thoughts.

For me and many others, leisure is difficult. What an absurd and funny paradox.

This chapter is about nurturing relationships, becoming comfortable with who you are, and enjoying the ride.

"Life moves pretty fast. If you don't stop and look around once in a while, you could miss it." -Ferris Bueller

How to kill **boredom** in traffic.

Call your ol' pal Schmidt.

Listen to Elon Musk **podcast** about eradicating traffic.

Leave car and **walk** to Chuck E. Cheese.

Cool outfits to wear at the **smoking bar.**

Telltale signs it's time to **look for a new job.**

YOU'RE ON EDGE MORE THAN YOU'RE NOT.

WAKING UP IS DAUNTING OR KIND OF A BUMMER.

IF YOU TAKE CALCULATED RISKS, ODDS ARE YOU'LL LAND ON YOUR FEET.

THE PEOPLE AROUND
YOU ARE MAKING
YOU **SAD.**

CIG BREAKS
ARE EXCITING.

TIME STANDS STILL

THE BAR
IS THE ONLY
ESCAPE.

Sweet ways to quit your job.

Take out the trash
and keep walking.

Write a
letter of resignation
on a cake

Drive to
Lollapalooza instead.

Change the letters
on the sign.

If the company
needs public shaming,
make a song and
put it on Spotify.

"You've gotta fight
for your right to party."
-Beastie Boys

Uses for bananas other than consumption.

Make bullies slip when they give chase

Bitch slap cheating boyfriend

Mario Kart

Ways to make **exercise** more fun.

Jog in an area
where there is action.

Listen to mind-stimulating
podcasts in the
weightroom.

Dance poorly to favorite
records at home.

Pretend you're in
a video game
while biking.

The hardest part about going for a jog is **getting out the door.**

HENRY ROLLINS

Non-mainstream **dance** moves

THE
JACKHAMMER

THE
T-REX

THE LEBRON JAMES

THE
SWIM SWIM

THE
KARATE MASTER

THE
ROGER CLEMENS

THE
CLOWN TOWN

THE
LIZARD MAN.

THE
PTERODACTYL

SCREECH!

People get excited about moves they've never seen before.

How to find more excitement in life.

OPTION 1

Chase tornadoes
in a convertible.

OPTION 2

Watch "Twister" with
Bill Paxton on cable.

inspired by my bud peter christensen

How to **Age** gracefully

Shave your head.

Buy a really dumb, ironic t-shirt.

Host a garage party.

Eat termites because apparently they make you immortal in some cultures.

How to decide what to watch on **Netflix.**

Ask most reliable friend.

Close eyes and enter cheat code to **Super Mario Bros 3**

Exciting part-time job idea.

OPTION

Get a job picking up
golf balls.

BETTER OPTION

Dodge the golf balls
that patrons hit at you.

How to start a **cult.**

Grow a beard.

Provide
free drinks.

Recite lines from
"Back to the Future"
at high volumes.

Popular **questions** you'll get if you choose to pursue the **arts**.

Advice is good, but don't ask
more than 2-3 people or your brain
will **implode**.

Signals our parents are trying to **connect** with us...

Mom continually **texts** you about Netflix programming options.

Your **dad** pokes you aggressively and yells friendly stuff.

How ya doin buddy!

Your **mom** recites the weather report in your direction.

Sunny n stuff

DURING THE FIRST FEW YEARS OF DOING SOMETHING **NEW**,

IT'S NORMAL TO FEEL LIKE A COMPLETE FRAUD.

(Even the **best** in the world have had "**imposter syndrome**.")

If you want to start something new,
odds are you'll land on your feet
if you have a good head on your shoulders.

Why you should fly your **freak flag.**

IT'S CATHARTIC

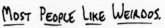

MOST PEOPLE LIKE WEIRDOS.

☐ NO PEOPLE
☐ SOME PEOPLE
☑ MOST PEOPLE
☐ ALL PEOPLE

ONLY BULLIES WILL MAKE FUN OF YOU.

LOSER!

(a bully's opinion is negate of value)

BEING NORMAL ISN'T THAT FUN.

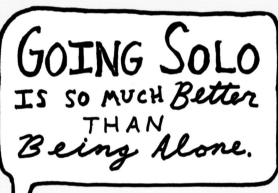

"SCENE CRED"
Based on winter hat size.

LOSER

Wear a
large, warm hat
that actually
protects
your ears

NOT
RELEVANT

Wear a
medium-sized
hat

HIP

Wear your hat
like a yamaka
and get frostbite
to impress
your scene

A few good ways to fly your **freak flag.**

Wear a wolf shirt.

Wear a karate suit in public.

Listen to whatever makes you feel good.

Hang out with fellow weirdos.

Attend a conference in your niche

Great cities for
escaping normal.

NEW ORLEANS

AUSTIN TX

ASHEVILLE, NC

PORTLAND, OR

BERLIN,

Hey, don't forget Savannah, Georgia!

If you feel trapped,
explore new things in your city.

GREAT STAND UP COMEDY NIGHTS.

Milwaukee, WI (my city)

CRAZY OLD BASILICA MODELED AFTER ST PETERSBURG, RUSSIA

SUMMER CONCERT SERIES.

SWEET BIKE TRAILS EVERYWHERE.

HISTORIC OLD BUILDINGS UNTOUCHED BY TIME.

CLASSIC ARCADE.

Fun items to always keep in your car.

FRISBEE

SHORTS + RUNNING SHOES.

CHEAP GUITAR

WEIGHTS
DUMB BELLS OR KETTLEBELLS

SOCCER BALL

HORSE MASK
(Just kidding, you don't need this)

Sweet **places** to write a song, poem, essay, journal, drawing or maybe anything...

LAUNDROMAT

AIRPLANE

PARK BENCH

COFFEE SHOP
(AKA "caffeine store")

SIDEWALK IN A PUBLIC PLACE.

COOL MOTEL

Sweet places for unblocking **writer's block.**

BOOKSTORE

RECORD SHOP

Final Thoughts

Hello person.

Thank you for reading ***IT'S HARD TO BE A PERSON: Defeating Anxiety, Surviving the World and Having More Fun***. This is basically the end of the book.

If you've enjoyed this book, please pass it along to a buddy. Hopefully it'll be useful to more persons.

I hope to meet you out on the road sometime. I'm usually out touring with my band and we typically hang out after shows. Here is where we will be: *www.brettnewski.com/tour*

Also, if you'd like updates on new books, shows, podcasts or just want to ask a question, feel free to email me at *hardtobeaperson@gmail.com*

Much love and respect,
-Newski

ODDS N' ENDS

Notebook stuff I made when I was bored...

WILLIE NELSON IS...

☐ COOL
☐ RAD
☐ SWEET
☑ DOPE

CHUCK RAGAN ... BRETT NEWSKI

SNEEZY

SLEEPY

HAPPY

GRUMPY

DOPEY

BASHFUL

NEWSKI

DAVE GROHL

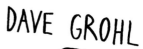

IS MY DAD.

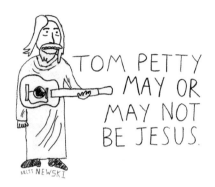

what people are saying about newski's latest album...

mega fun tour this was...

t-shirt ideas

Advice for bands....

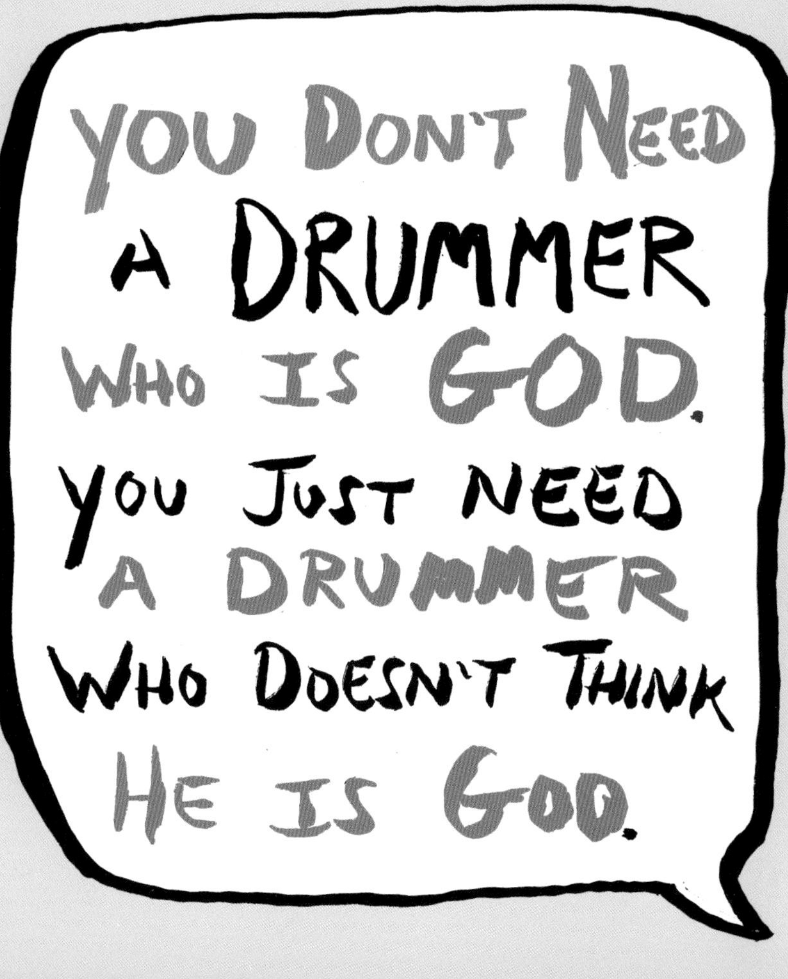

How to get discovered at **SXSW**

Light yourself on fire.

DIRT FROM THE ROAD PODCAST

Musicians and comedians tell their strangest stories from the road, share mental health boosts, and navigate the hurdles of being a person in modern times.

Guests include *The Lumineers, Dashboard Confessional, Frank Turner, Joe List, Charlie Berens, Toad the Wet Sprocket, Verve Pipe, All American Rejects* and more.

*Available wherever you listen to pods.

Other stuff I've made...

It's Hard to be a Person: soundtrack to the book! (2021)

While rummaging thru my parents basement,
I found notebooks of old lyrics from growing up
and trying to figure it all out. I adapted these
notebooks into new songs that fit well with the book.

"There is no fear in getting lost if you're doing it on purpose" shirt

AKA the rocketship shirt. First shirt I ever did
draw. The lyric is from a song I made called
"Corazones on Cobblestones." It's about being alone
really far from home, which can be brutally lonely
but it's also the most free feeling you can achieve.

Life Upside Down (2018, LP or CD)

This is an anti-anxiety album. It's melodic indie-alt
music and the songs are really short and
to-the-point. Recorded to analog tape in Oakland,
CA this is the album people have bought the most
times. Spatola played all the bass and drums.

...more stuff I've made...

Failed Hipster shirt

Keeping track of trends is too much work. Give up. Proudly rep your failure to hipsterdom & support arts n culture with this fine Bella Canvas shirt.

Don't Let the Bastards Get You Down (2020, LP or CD)

How do you feel when someone starts playing on their phone while you're talking to them? It's a dark moment. This album tackles the erosion of face-to-face human connection, the breakdown of the proverbial village, the destruction of the planet, and the myriad ways in which our social media addictions amplify these problems.

Don't Listen to Brett Newski shirt

Because there is already way too much music in the world to keep track of.

https://brettnewski.com/merch

Land Air Sea Garage (2016, LP or CD)

Our German record label hated half the songs, so we ended up recording 5 new tracks on-the-fly while in the woods in Sri Lanka. Melodic rock album with a fan favorite song called "DIY", which is about playing the worst show of my entire life where the St Louis "crowd" wanted me dead.

Personal canvas painting of you, a friend, family member or mortal enemy

Sometimes I personally draw and paint a custom canvas for folks. Delivered to you in the mail.

American Folk Armageddon (2014, LP or CD)

I wrote most of this album while living in Saigon, Vietnam from 2011-2013. It is my first official release and Good Land Records put it out. Recommended if you like Violent Femmes, Mountain Goats, Ben Kweller, or hard-driving acoustic music.

https://brettnewski.com/merch

If you'd like to further support this project,
the absolute best way is to join my **Patreon** :)

www.patreon.com/brettnewski1

I can't stress enough how vital this platform
has been in keeping the ship afloat. Thank you.

BRETT NEWSKI is an alternative songwriter, podcaster and illustrator based in Milwaukee, Wisconsin. He hosts a weekly **podcast** called **Dirt from the Road**; where musicians and comedians tell their strangest road stories and share mental health boosting tips.

His work has been featured in **Rolling Stone, NPR, American Songwriter, PopMatters, Boston Globe & SiriusXM.**

Find more at:
https://brettnewski.com/